japanese motorcycles

japanese
100 hp/11 sec./150 mph
motorcycles

Tim Parker

Osprey Colour Series

Published in 1985 by Osprey Publishing Limited
12–14 Long Acre, London WC2E 9LP
Member company of the George Philip Group

British Library Cataloguing in Publication Data
Parker, Tim
    Japanese motorcycles.—(Osprey colour series)
    1. Motorcycles, Japanese—Pictorial works
    I. Title
    629.2'275'0952   TL440
ISBN 0-85045-647-9

Printed in Italy

Contents

1 Biggest, but are they best? – HONDA   8

2 The smallest are known for strength – KAWASAKI   36

3 Can be mighty on their day – SUZUKI   65

4 Both front runner and follower – YAMAHA   94

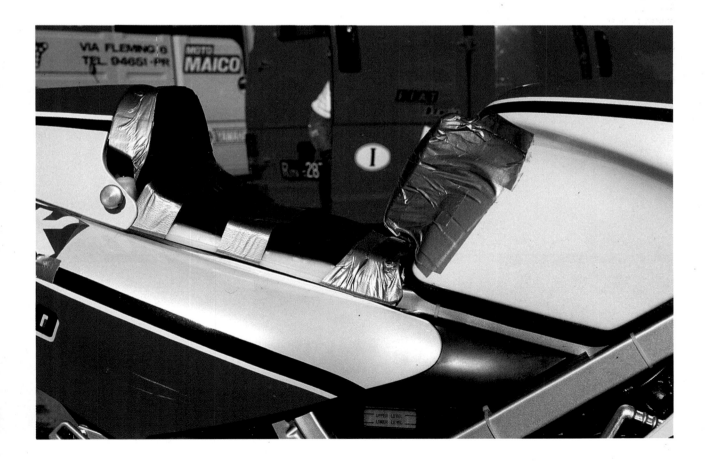

During 1984 I had the good fortune to be able to ride a large number of the then current crop of Japanese high performance sports motorcycles, all on loan from the British importers of the Big Four. Thus I must first of all extend my grateful thanks to all those who listened to my pleading and trusted me with their charges. They each knew all along that the excuse of taking photographs of their machinery was really pretty thin, riding was what it was all about.

I'm also indebted to a number of others who helped me including George Magnus, John Parker, Gerald Foster, the insurance broker, Bassano, Andrew Morland, Martin and Judy Parsley and Chloe. Simpson helmet (with obligatory Bell sticker to throw off the scent of the British police, for this excellent piece of equipment is not street legal here), Highwayman leathers, Alpinestar boots and Bates gloves all helped to save my skin. Minolta, then Canon, Kodak and Fuji took care of the rest.

Apart from the photographic aspect, I learnt a lot. To sum up, I learnt to ride street fast in a way that I have never previously achieved riding Italian motorcycles for the past ten years. I gained a new awareness and this necessitated that I thoroughly review my feelings about 'the Japanese motorcycle'.

I experienced holding the speedometer needle hovering around 155 mph aboard a Kawasaki 900 on a motorway – I felt safe. I was happily winding a Yamaha RD500LC through London traffic in the pouring rain without concern – this machine has so much character; perhaps I should say 'these two machines, in one'. I recall the very usefulness of the Suzuki 1100 Katana – so powerful and easily ridden, and all in perhaps Japan's only real attempt at radical styling, albeit from a European drawing board.

Times have changed. There is charisma, character and so much genuine riding pleasure to be had in many of these bikes. This book offers only a passing review of some of what was most exciting in 1984, although some of my shots were both earlier and later. It works within a rough definition of '100 hp/11 sec./150 mph', if not a definition of reality, then certainly one which can be applied to the bike 'standing still'.

In 1985, of course, we already see 120 hp/10 sec./160 mph looming. Maybe another book? Enjoy this great styling and technical revolution.

Tim Parker

1 Biggest, but are they best? - HONDA

Right Real performance undoubtedly comes with this Honda 1000 CBX 6-cylinder engined special shot at the Imola race track in Italy in 1985. The frame maker is unknown but he has done a good job with a lot of triangulation and bracing near the steering head. Note the 16-inch front wheel, trick bodywork and magnesium race-spec. Brembo brakes.

Unfortunately Honda themselves didn't have great sales success with their superb 6-cylinder production machines. It seemed that no one really wanted six cylinders when four or less would do. Neither Kawasaki nor Benelli have had real success with their sixes either

Below Something else to be done with a CBX engine. This one, shot in Woodland Hills, north of Los Angeles, is turbocharged – no power figures quoted. Various kits are available for such an application when 'overkill' is needed. The rotor and exhausts seem to fit happily in the standard frame

Below Honda's turbo attempt at high performance. The CX650 Turbo followed the CX500 version. Very powerful but not totally successful. *Right* Another Honda Turbo shot at the Rock Store, Mulholland Highway, next to a V4 500 Interceptor

Above Honda's standard amongst 'universal Japanese motorcycles' or UJMs, a phrase almost certainly coined by some West Coast motorcycle journalist, is the CB900F, first catalogued in Japan in 1980. This followed the CB750F with the double overhead camshaft four, which succeeded the original single cam CB750. This one shot at Mallory Park race circuit is pretty stock and looks to be of 1981 vintage. This popular model doesn't have 150 mph potential

Right A 1982 CB900F with special paint, rear sets and custom seat plus exhaust, swing arm, rear suspension units and front fork brace. Shot at Mallory Park as an infiltrator during a Laverda Owners Club meeting

Left CB900F double overhead cam across-the-frame four has not become as popular as the other similar engines from Suzuki and Kawasaki, thus this tuned version by Ontario Moto Tech of North Hollywood is rare. Silver foil protects the inlet stacks from foreign bodies with this fine set of Keihin smoothbore 'CR' carburettors, an essential modification for such an engine

Above CB1100R – this well used production racing version is an example of a stunningly fast, virtually factory race-replica machine homologated and then sold out of the showroom solely with racing in mind. Successful they were – at least in Britain, both on road and track. Expensive too. In one way, at least, these were the start of the mega-performance bike

Left A lovely example of the CB1100F which has obviously only ever been used on the street. These machines were very popular in Italy – this one was shot in the paddock during the Italian Grand Prix at Misano in 1984. Replica bodywork was soon available to enable CB750 and 900Fs to pose

Above British enthusiast rides his CB1100R during a test day at Mallory Park. This one has a change in exhaust compared with the previous machines

French frame manufacturer Moto Martin has supplied a large number of frames for Honda engines into the UK, mostly through south London dealer Mocheck. This Honda powered machine offers monoshock rear suspension for the CB750 or 900 across-the-frame four-cylinder engine

Honda went V4 in 1982 whilst most others stayed with the straight across-the-frame four in some form or other, except when it came to the large touring cruisers. This is a VF750S shot in Italy at the Monza track in early 1984. The track was being used for an historic car race – in the background is a Porsche Carrera and the tail of a Lotus 21 sticking out. Early camshaft problems hit this ultimately successful engine

Honda Britain's 1984 VF750F-E road test machine shot in two locations in central London. Buckingham Palace at 6.30 a.m. is no place to be except that traffic won't be there either. A side road in the attractive part of Chiswick, Bedford Park, is the location for the other, in front of a Citroen CX2400. The Citroen is considered to be an acquired art for any driver, as is the Honda.

Many heralded the VF750F or Interceptor (in the USA) as the answer to all their sports roadster problems. Perhaps its complexity has put many off.

In the right hands, it's a joy to ride with its 16 in. front wheel and super stiff chassis. In 1983 it had the strongest engine available in a 750

Race prepared VF750F as used by the Rothmans
Honda Britain team in 1985 for the new Superstock
series of racing. This formula was essentially created in
America by Bruce Cox to revive 'production' racing.
This is ace rider Roger Marshall's machine ready for
the first race in the series at Brands Hatch on Good
Friday, in April 1985. The VF750F was hard pressed
to stay with either the Suzuki GSX-R750 or Yamaha
FZ750

Not a super high performance bike, this Honda 650 Nighthawk. But a nice shot of a truly lovely motorcycle taken at the Rock Store outside Los Angeles. As a blacktop cruiser it couldn't be better; faster than you think too

Above Whilst Britain was seeing the chain drive across-the-frame CBX750F out and out sports roadster, America was being offered the 750 Nighthawk S. The Nighthawk came in Californian hot rod style but with shaft drive – still the same 16-valve, hydraulic valve adjustment system double overhead camshaft engine. The one horrible snippet is the fake velocity stack showing through each side – better to paint those black!

Goleta's Honda shop just north of Santa Barbara, in California provided this example

This racing may not feature 150 mph motorcycles but it is fast and exciting. This is Honda's *Trofeo Monomarca* VF400F, the round at the Italian Grand Prix, at Misano in 1984, actually the second in that year's six round competition. The bikes have to be stock, plus factory offered race kit, and then ridden like hell. Here's the start

American market V65 Magna provides real muscle but in a custom package. The shot was taken at one Sunday brunch time. California light almost guarantees a happy shot. The V65 Magna comes with 1098 cc V4 engine with 6-speed shaft drive transmission and not excessive weight at 542 lb dry. Apart from great flexibility making those six speeds superfluous, the Magna has tyre ripping characteristics described by *Cycle* magazine as eyeball-flattening

V65 Sabre with fairing at the Rock Store. The Sabre differs from the Magna essentially in styling and suspension. The Magna has the traditional twin rear shock swing arm set up whilst the Sabre has Honda's monoshock Pro-Link air-assisted rear, and front TRAC anti-dive, and can thus be blasted through canyons at speeds in excess of those that its looks suggest

For those who like maximum power all packaged in a
hot rod style, the V65 Sabre should be an answer. The
slim 1100 V4 engine delivers the power from its just
over-square bore and stroke ratio, and massive power
it is too. Couple this with the sobre, non-flash
paintwork and it becomes a real sleeper. Dry weight is
only 532 lb and so, within excess of 100 horsepower,
the rear tyre doesn't last long.

Side by side is a Suzuki GS850E, a much more
unsurprising machine

Cam gear drive V4 Honda VF1000R shot at Box Hill, famous collecting place for Sunday motorcyclists, just close to Dorking in Surrey in 1984. The 1000R's engine is special to it with its long train of cam drive gears (instead of chain) and its bore and stroke of 77 × 53.6 mm for 998 cc. The 1000F, without the street racer's bodywork, comes with a not dissimilar engine, but no gear drive.

Note 16 in. front and 17 in. rear wheels and fully floating discs. This bike is serious, just like the CB1100R which it superseded, and it too is in short supply, expensive and fast

Two VF1000Rs together, a rare sight. Where else but Italy? Actually at Imola in 1985 for the Imola 200 (won by miles by American Eddie Lawson on his factory Yamaha). This model, unlike its predecessor, is now available on the US market and similarly will be vastly expensive in every market. Its price puts it ahead of the field by quite a long way, with both the Kawasaki 900 Ninja and Yamaha FJ1100 some 25 per cent or so cheaper, and yet it is questionable whether it is either much faster or more stable than either. Lovely though it is, its rarity must be its major virtue

All the current trick features come with the swoopy
VF1000R – square tube, silver coated frame, frame top
mounted fuel tank with modern dial-type fuel tap,
cannister style exhausts, full race-style fairing, single
seat with dualseat option and more. Moody shot
somewhere in Italy

Brand new, straight off the showroom floor the day
before, this VF500 (Interceptor in the US market and
some others) started its running-in by be)ng ridden to
the Rock Store, outside Los Angeles. Many consider
this middleweight V4 Honda sports machine as the
very best of its kind. Comparatively priced with a
remarkable spread of usable power (73 hp from its
498 cc, only weighing 409 lb dry) through its six-speed
gearbox, the mini Interceptor works well

Left Here's the Italian market VF500F photographed in early 1984 outside the Misano circuit entrance amongst a large Honda Italia display. Precise styling, paintwork and bodywork specifications vary around the world – one can seldom be absolutely sure what's what. For example, note the all black Comstar wheels on this bike compared with the polished and black wheels on the bike in the previous photograph

Above 1985 version of the VF500FII comes with full fairing and more style. Essentially the 56 in. wheelbase (some three inches shorter than its bigger brother the VF750F – now VF700F in the USA) chassis and strong engine are unaltered leaving the near 130 mph capability and quick steering yet stunning handling much as before. This was taken at Imola, close to Bologna, the home of Ducati

2 The smallest are known for strength- KAWASAKI

Kawasaki have long been known for high performance motorcycles, and in the beginning with the stunning three-cylinder two strokes and then the original 900 Z1 and subsequent clones, for unstable handling. Things have changed dramatically in the 1980s, not only have performance levels changed but so have those flexiframes! Early GPz1100 was part of that revolution – massive horsepower with the beginnings of chassis control

As was the previous photograph, this 'Eddie Lawson Replica' was shot at the Rock Store (LA, CA). Whilst the GPz range went one way in styling and became a proper range with a variety of engine sizes, the Z1000R maintained more traditional style and went 'hot rod' instead, following the sit up and beg, straight bar racer that Eddie rode so successfully for Kawasaki in American AMA Superbike racing. The Kerker pipe was US stock for the 'R' and these interesting machines were kept in short supply

Above Digital fuel injection for Kawasaki's behemoth ZG1300 6-cylinder, water cooled giant. 130 hp for 135 mph, but only 30 mpg for this plain solo, weighing in at 600 lb plus. The engine is super smooth, and mighty powerful

Left A very neat, obviously carefully constructed Eddie Lawson Replica replica. Real straight bars, beefed-up swing arm, cannister exhaust and too much flat black single this one out. Steering damper and floating rear brake caliper show that necessity is the mother of invention! Shot at Box Hill, when the sun shone

Above Dinosaur amongst the dinosaurs. Gravel tip at Dronfield, near Sheffield in England's industrial midrift was a suitable stopping place to rest after wrestling with this 'big thing'. To maintain a fast road speed, a special technique is certainly required. It's mostly a question of sitting well forward and to the left, uncomfortable, yes, but safe. Shake, rattle and roll at any decent speed. Most markets would find the Z1300-6 packaged differently – in the USA, for example, that means the ZN1300 Voyager (in 1985), a thoroughly nice Honda Gold Wing competitor. Come to that, a 'stripped' Gold Wing is much easer to live with

Above right Achieve today's speeds with yesterday's rugged machinery. The Performance Works, Canoga Park in the San Fernando Valley (CA) specializes in conversions (remanufacturing, they'd prefer) – here's 120 hp and 150 mph potential in a 1979 Kawasaki Z1000 MkII, the bike 'where the high speed handling stopped being terrifying' (*Motorcycle International*). C/r trans., 1105 Moriwaki single ring slipper pistons, big valves, custom made exhaust, 29 mm carbs., PW cams, Morris mags, Hunt alloy discs, Grimeca calipers and much, much more

Right GPz1100 – massive straightline performance

40

IT MAY LEAD YOU INTO TEMPTATION

THE CAMRY 2.0 GLi. TO

Above GPz1100 (Kawasaki's own nomenclature is ZX1100-A2) in May 1984. The instrument panels on this series of GPzs has taken a lot of criticism – wrong sizes and in the wrong places. This bike's speed saw 140 mph – steady – two up on occasion when the road was straight, smooth and deserted

Left In mid-1984 there was a campaign afloat to disfigure advertisements which might possibly persuade one to buy goods for the wrong reasons . . . in the case of cars, the wrong reason was 'speed' or 'power' or 'machismo'. This Toyota advertisement on route to London's Heathrow Airport escaped long enough to shoot this GPz1100 in front. The 1100 was more a temptress than the Camry ever could be

43

GPz1100 with 120 hp capable of 145 mph and 11 second quarter miles is both peaky in its power delivery via fuel injection and sometimes strange to handle through the corners – care is needed! Straightline stability can never be questioned, though, neither can rider comfort.

For those who like the feel of a big bike combined with the reality, the GPz1100 is still a major contender

Right The big Kawasaki double overhead camshaft, across-the-frame UJM four cylinder engine is considered bulletproof, and if not actually unburstable, close to it. Together with Suzuki's directly competitive motor the Big Ks are terribly popular for those who desire more performance still. The GPz1100 engine of 1089 cc from a bore and stroke of 72.5 × 66 mm is perhaps the last of the big bruisers – pre-high tech. – which run air-cooled, two-valve, chain drive cams and convention. Fuel injection pointed a presently 'no through road' to more power

Below GPz1100 – still the 'F-4 Phantom of the pavement' (*Cycle*). Nearly as much money is spent these days on a motorcycle's graphics as it is on its chassis – well, nearly!

Right GPz550 and GPz750, both conventional UJMs, are nevertheless still very competitive and handsome motorcycles. This GPz550 comes as ZX550A1 whereas the equivalent GPz750 is the ZX750A2

Near 130 mph, 12.4 second quarter mile, and one of the sweetest and best balanced engine and chassis combinations one can buy. No super sophisticated components, just well-worked and compatible, and all in a dry weight of 481 lb. The ZX750A2 GPz is still worthy, particularly competitively priced in the USA inspite of being more than 700 cc, because this model is assembled in Lincoln, Nebraska – in a word it delivers without complication.

For everyday, it licks the new generation 750s into a cocked hat.

This shot was taken in a delightful west London street where kids still play in safety and peace

Above Perhaps the only successful, truly successful in both operational and financial terms, production turbo motorcycle – the ZX750 Turbo. Based on the already highly prized (and praised) GPz750, the Turbo is both less complex and faster than Honda's, Suzuki's or Yamaha's answers to the turbo question. In its day the 'Kwacker Puffer' was virtually the fastest thing going with 122 hp and only 514 dry pounds to push (sorry, blow) along.

How much 'real' difference is there when compared with the un-blown GPz750 – for the Turbo: 26 hp, 33 lb more in weight, nine mph, 0.9 of a second in the quarter. Decide for yourself

Left Glorious red and black paint pinpoint the 750 Turbo away from the GPz550's grey, here, at a dull Brands Hatch race meeting in 1985

While the buying public stayed away from the
competition's turbos, they flocked for a time to
Kawasaki's. This rain soaked example needed right
wrist caution to reach its parking spot at the Bath and
West Showground in England's deepest West Country
for a custom and classic bike show. Already there are
turbo collectors . . .

Harris makes a lovely handmade frame to envelope a
number of engines – here's a rather garish example
shot at Brands Hatch in early 1985 using an early dohc
Kawasaki engine. There was a time not so long ago
that the only answer to true high performance
handling and low weight was to throw away the
standard Japanese frame and use the delicious power
unit in something like a Harris tailor-made chassis.
Today, unless total individuality is required, the
standard frame is more than good enough.

Nevertheless so-called special building still flourishes
as individuality reigns and there is a plentiful supply of
engines – from old or crashed machines

German special building is a high tech. industry all of
its own. This Jung-framed Kawasaki photographed at
the Cologne Show in late 1984 already exhibits a host
of racing style components, many of which will
become *de rigueur* on production street bikes. To hell
with the expense . . .

Above No one understood why Kawasaki followed the GPz1100 and 750 Turbo, their two flag ships in 1983, with a 900, until they saw it and rode it. The ZX900, or GPz900R, or Ninja had the weight of the old 750 and the performance of the old 1100. Wonderful, wonderful motorcycle with gallons (or litres) of character as these Italian *piloti* soon discovered on their ride into the Dolomite foothills not far from Bassano del Grappa, actually Laverda country

Right Imola, April 1985 and the rain was looming. It didn't come. Suddenly the Ninja was the bike to be seen on in Italy. Sales exceeded all reasonable bounds

Two Ninjas at the Rock Store. 1984 colours were blue
or red in the USA and most other markets, but not in
Britain. The Ninja engine is indeed special. It's water
cooled, very slim because all the ancilleries are parked
behind the block and because the chain driving the
double overhead camshafts is on one end, and features
four valves per cylinder, coupled with a six speed
transmission. The 908 cc engine is over square and can
thus rev healthily to 10,500 before the red line looms.
92 horsepower results. One secret for its uncanny
smoothness and controllability is the counterbalancer,
unique to across-the-frame fours. Perhaps for the very
first time, Kawasaki also have an excellent chassis, to
provide superb road holding, ride, steering and
braking. It's just that good

Choice of the Ninja name was clever, but why is it not used in every market? Rumour has it that the similarly styled GPz750R is even smoother than the 900 and that there is a new 'super-Ninja' on the way; 1000 or 1100? Also that there's a new 750 to compete directly with the new super fast Suzuki and Yamaha, even an upcoming Honda

Above Build quality whilst not to Bimota standard is very high indeed these days with the 'new generation' Japanese superfast sportsters. Note Shaw filler style racing fuel cap, now expected on every machine

Overleaf left At rest in Plymouth, close to where Sir Francis Drake bowled, having run 93 miles in no time at all. Excessively high average speeds are possible with an experienced solo rider, even if the roads are damp. *Right* The same road test machine in Swansea dock, in South Wales, after a long ride west from London. Neither side nor head winds affect this supreme roadster much. Here, perhaps, is the ultimate unfussy touring, commuting motorcycle capable of 150 mph – at least, today

Below Will the Kawasaki GPz600R be the best middleweight? Some say it will, others say, competent that it is, it's characterless where the Ninja is so strong. The mini-Ninja, though, uses essentially an uprated GPz550 engine but with 16 valves and water or liquid cooling. Cam chain drive is still in the middle. In other words it isn't a 'new generation' engine, yet. This ultra-fast (135 mph, 12.13 sec. quarter) 75 hp, 430 dry lb sportster can play the game for you. Shot here in Cologne in late 1984

3 Can be mighty on their day-SUZUKI

Bottom right Amongst the brothers at the Rock Store
one Sunday, this double overhead camshaft but two
valve GS1000 with S-type handlebar fairing Suzuki
lurks through. The two valve dohc GS1000 series
made between 1978 and 1981 (S with fairing was 1980,
and more normally with blue and white stripes) must
still be considered mighty by anyone for whom it isn't
essential to have the latest piece of high tech. or big
engined exotica

Customized GS1000R at Mallory Park in 1984 waiting to 'blow off' various Laverdas and other Italian machinery. The R came with the rectangular headlamp which many didn't like compared with the previous round headlamp also available at the time. Strong engines these, plenty are still around and they are favourable priced, and thus they are popular with hot rodders. Handling can be predictable with care, especially with uprated shocks, good European tyres and a steering damper

GSX – the next generation of big bore Suzukis, this time with double overhead cams and four-valve heads. Well known for their unburstable qualities. For 1981 when production commenced, the GSX was ahead of the Honda and Kawasaki competition. . . .
Above Making the best of unstylish styling, this tricked out GSX1100 must be an improvement. Box Hill, near Dorking, Surrey. *Right* Same basic motorcycle, different interpretation, this time at Mallory Park

Above Yet another GSX1100, again at Box Hill. Reliant Robin on the left is often known as the 'plastic pig', stylingwise that might be appropriate for the GSX, except that the power of its engine would be too much for any pig

Right Black GS1100E to American spec. – in the UK the X suffix would have been added to the GS – in its day the best value tarmac scorcher money could buy. Uncomplicated styling and that big headlamp – up amongst the mountains past the Rock Store on Mulholland Highway

Left The next generation of GS or GSX 1100s, but with much, much better styling. The ES suffix means the short fairing. A further E would mean a full fairing. Complicated? Still straightforward, though, are the mechanicals as performance is increased still further. These big Suzukis soon became outdated with the Uni-Trak Kawasakis and the V4 Hondas, but they hung on well because of their raw power

Above GSX1100S Katana first hit the world in 1981. A lovely heavyweight engine in a good attempt at a European sportster frame, plus European sourced by Japanese produced styling. Not everyone likes its looks, and today they may even be passé, but there's no questioning the ridability of the total machine.

Strange instruments counter rotate

Left Well used road tester worked very, very well. Shot from a strange angle in west London. Remarkably easy to ride although it's a big machine, the 1100 Katana has sold remarkably well and should one day become a classic motorcycle worth preserving. High tech. looks but actually simple mechanicals

Below Part of the cleverness. Sensible choke lever position, easy access to the fuses and no superfluous panelling or gizmos. Low bars and slightly rearset footrest provide reasonable rider and pillion comfort. The bike's a firm favourite with drag and circuit racers

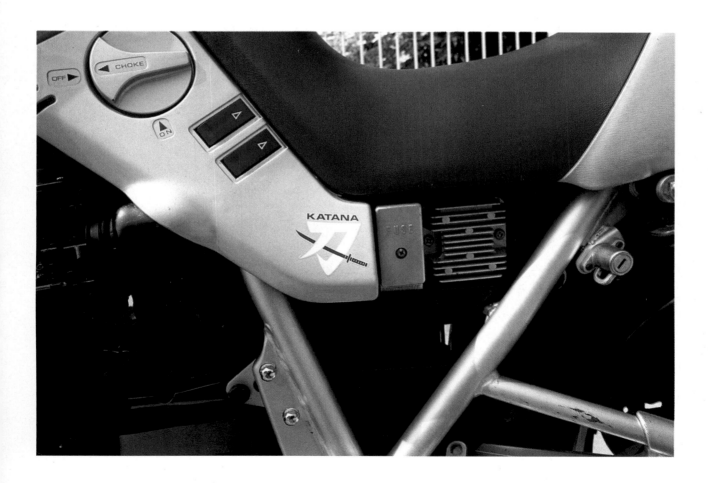

Above Silly mirrors but what else are Suzuki to do? Look at clever and subtle use of colour on the seat and elsewhere. The other Katana models worked less well from a styling viewpoint. There's a more modern version currently in Japan (750 engine, though) with a flip-up headlamp cover. This one looks really menacing

Right Brand new Katana – still good value – at High Beech in Epping Forest, north of London, another favourite riding haunt for Sunday joyriders. Where simplicity counts, still an important motorcycle with near 140 mph capability. Once more, you either like the styling or you don't, there's no middle way

The Katana 1100 was and is a serious production racing machine with considerable speed, great reliability and predictable handling. Important too, is that the bike is tough and easy to work on. Riding position and general track suitability is built-in, fortunately.

This is the October meeting at Silverstone – a production machine race with competitors waiting to get out onto the track – at which high speed trials are run. Thirty minutes of blasting one of these can cause fatigue!

Note crankcase safety bars – such is the cut and thrust of production racing, one must be prepared to fall over occasionally

Above Working out the type numbers of 1984 Suzukis is not easy. This is a GSX550EFE to British 1984 spec. In the USA one like this would be a GS550ESE but wouldn't have the full fairing. In the UK, if it didn't have the full fairing but only the half fairing, it would lose its last E. Oh well, it's complicated, and what's written on the bike isn't necessarily what it's called. For 1985 nothing much changed in the UK but in the USA there was the choice of the same half fairing and a new handlebar fairing.

Power across the water in north Kent

Right Victorian houses in south London offer suitable backdrop for this thoroughly modern but not now high tech. Suzuki. The 550 will run close to 125 mph on its tough and smooth across-the-frame, air-cooled 4-cylinder pumping out 65 hp. Handling is a little skitty, though

Left For some reason best known to themselves, Japanese manufacturers have been telling the world what their particular bike has in the way of features – not just in their advertising or brochures, but actually all over the machines themselves.

Suzuki used some restraint with their 'Full Floater Suspension'. Take a look at some of the others, though

Above GSX750EF ready to run at Brands Hatch in the first British Superstock race on Good Friday in 1985. Unfortunately last year's technology didn't allow this machine to run competitively with the very latest water-cooled hot shots.

With 84 horsepower and only 463 lb dry, this 750 will show a healthy 130 mph on the street. It does have state of the art suspension, though, coupled with a now 'behind' engine spec.

Below Happy Italian rider with his GSX750EF at Imola in 1985. As a road-going 750, this machine is second to none and benefits from simplicity. The new racer-replica GSX-R750 may prove too twitchy on the road

Right Harry Maillet of The Performance Works, in Canoga Park, CA, also wheeled out this 1982 GS1100 (GSX in the UK) now converted to ES spec. This lovely machine epitomizes what can be done with careful custom work. Would you believe 128 hp at the rear wheel? Just note the neat tricks

Pity about Suzuki's turbo effort, the 672 cc XN85.
Didn't sell well enough. It's a complicated installation
which only really gave 750 performance (coupled with
dreadful fuel consumption) but in a nice set of cycle
parts. The colour scheme didn't help, either.
Backwater. Shot in Santa Barbara, California – they are
rare on the street

Race prepared road-going Bimotas are a rare sight. Expense is one thing, lack of suitable racing formulae is another – do they work well enough, is perhaps a third?

This one, Suzuki powered SB4, was spotted lurking in The Performance Works works about to be fettled for Tom Chastine to race West Coast in F1. This one comes with 1140 cc Yoshi pistons, and cams, and custom Kerker exhaust. The frame was acid dipped for lightness. A new swing arm completes the mods, although there is still not room for a large enough rear slick

Bimota's SB5 at Cologne in late 1984. Note pillion seat
hump cover and Bimota's own latest split rim wheels.

The Bimota is perhaps the best of what many
people might call 'specials'. Unfortunately for them,
the Japanese manufacturers have caught them up – not
in build quality or necessarily trick ideas – with a
performance/styling/price package that is impossible to
beat. Grab one of these beauties while you can

American pensioner, straight from the store, ignores
Suzuki's mega hot rod, the GS1150ESE in this Santa
Barbara dealer's window. With this model Suzuki
overbored their stomping 4-valve 1100 to 1135 cc and
gave it a Full-Floater single stock rear end. Also came
a longer wheelbase and new cams. Handling is
excellent and the engine strongly competitive with any
of the other high speed, high tech. machinery of that
size

In Britain the 'same' bike came as the GSX1100EF but with full fairing, 1135 cc and 122 horsepower, but with a dry weight of 543 lb and so much engine mid-range; the bike is fast if slightly overdone. All this means under 11 second standing quarters and around 145 mph top end. The whys and wherefores of two differently packaged motorcycles, in both the US and the UK, must remain a mystery

Above Nice road burner, two up, the fully faired GSX1100EF is. Road testing is no fun in the rain. When it isn't your motorcycle, its unfamiliarity and very size inhibit valid testing. Suffice to say, this mammoth is easy to handle provided the throttle is not twisted with sharpness

Then came the surprise from Suzuki. Having been without a super high tech. motorcycle at the top of their road-going production range, they landed the GSX-R750. Ready to race, at last a race bike you can ride on the road – a real racing bike, not just a replica – was on the lips of every well informed journalist. And, for once, it was true.

Here's one of the very first into the UK about to race at Brands Hatch in the first Superstock series event. This one was for journalist Roland Brown.

Thus this machine is stock, out of the crate, except for its Metzeler tyres and that steering damper looks to be extra

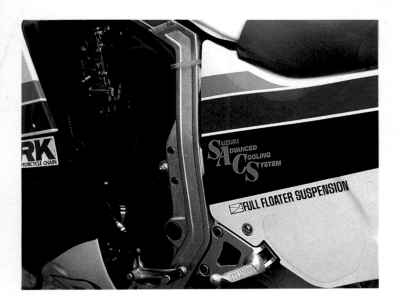

Above Novel technical feature of the GSX-R750 is that the engine is oil-cooled via SACS. In fact, it's the cylinder head which is cooled by a mass of engine oil being pumped through it, and cool it's kept. All this allows, Suzuki explains, for lighter and faster moving components. Claims for this delicious piece of trickery are 100 hp in a dry weight of under 400 lb. That means near 11 second quarters and nearly 150 mph – all from a 750!

Right First time out on the track in Britain (wet as usual, at Brands Hatch) veteran ace Mick Grant takes the GSX-R750 to an easy victory. The winning has gone on, too, for this machine

4 Both front runner and follower - YAMAHA

Beloved Elsie. Yamaha's phenomenally popular and outrageously fast (for a 350) RD350LC. *Below* A wet example at Box Hill. *Right* An illegal immigrant from Canada on Sunset Boulevard in Hollywood. They know what's good

After years of development with the air-cooled RDs, Yamaha went water-cooled just like the road racers. This is the second generation LC (for Liquid Cooled?), now with the YPVS engine, shot at Misano in 1984. Nearly 60 horsepower and a dry weight of around 320 lb means that this pocket rocket can deal with most machinery up to its top end of a neat 115 mph. Standing quarter comes out at just over 13 seconds

Right Ready for the race track, YPVS left and earlier LC right, at Mallory Park during a Laverda Owners Club test day. Man on the Laverda Jota, on their right, needs to worry for those two 350s will probably show him the way around that tight circuit.
　　Yamaha Pro-Am racing has been very popular especially as a relatively cheap form of road racing

Typical Yamaha Pro-Am racing machine at Brands
Hatch in early 1985. There's supposed to be very little
tuning, some race tyres are allowed (but not slicks),
and so many riders expend their energy in garish paint

Yamaha 1100 Midnight Special. Clever American
sourced marketing produced the all-black specials –
essentially factory customized production bikes to tease
your fantasies. In fact, these handsome machines were
a vast improvement in the regular 1100 shaft drive
beast that launched the company into the top of the
league of big bikes. These 1100 across-the-frame
Yamahas have vastly powerful engines but little chassis
refinement, at least in the earlier XS1100s

Right Two curious, vaguely unhappy motorcycles at Brands Hatch in 1985. On the left is Yamaha's turbo entry, their XJ750T, strangely styled, disappointing sportster. On the right is the Martini 'sponsored' XS1100 with its massive, British designed fairing.

There's power in the 1100 engine – massive torque, in fact – and the XJ650 without the turbo is a delightful machine, but as shown here . . .

Below Nicely styled Yamaha vee twin. Looks like the Italian market XV750 Virago in Midnight Special guise. It may not be super fast, but style and comfort reigns instead

With 90 horsepower on tap this should be some usable
motorcycle; unfortunately it doesn't seem to be that
way. For some the styling is harsh, for others the
reliability factor may just be too low. A better solution
to the turbo question that no one asked Yamaha was
to go for the non-turbo XJ750. This example was shot
north of Los Angeles and appeared to be regularly
used. Maybe all this is wrong . . .

Below XJ750 Yamaha four at Snetterton during a Classic Motor Cycle Racing Club event in 1984. The sun was shining! This upper-middle weight roadster suffers from handlebars which are too high but otherwise it's one of the best there is. With over 80 horsepower on tap, it's no mean performer even with its shaft drive. Racing versions have shown what can be done with this package, especially in Spain

Overleaf Posing Italians, something they love to do. Enthusiastic rider of the XJ750T hides one of Yamaha's superb XT600 Ténérés – very macho. The Ténéré pumps out 44 horsepower from its 595 cc and with a dry weight of around 300 lb, performs very well on the street. Some buy these dual purpose 'dirt bikes' for street use alone with their up-above-the-traffic stance

Above XJ750 engine is one of a family with a number of capacities around the 500, 600 and 750 size. Although understarred by similarly sized machines from the other three of the Big Four, these powerplants are strong and easy to live with. Their four-stroke technology is at least as advanced as their two stroke – as we shall see

Right 1984 was the year of two machines – no others were being talked about . . . well, perhaps less talked about. One of these was Yamaha's FJ1100. *Cycle* magazine said 'Yamaha's FJ1100 emerged as the benchmark machine'. *Motorcycle International* said 'Superb mile eater, just as good as the (Kawasaki) Ninja anywhere except on the track'. This one was photographed at the Rock Store

Left Evening sun in Shakespeare country. This road test machine was a pleasure to be with come rain or shine. Up to Birmingham on the motorway was a gallop, back through the countryside proper was both fast and safe. There is no better, or is it fortunately just equal first?

Above Second nature to passing Italians, here in Bassano del Grappa, is good design. No worry for them.

The FJ1100 comes with around 125 horsepower but nearly 560 lb dry, thus its speed is held to a whisker under 150 mph and standing quarters in the late 10s

Fun at Imola aboard a nearly new FJ1100. It's a pleasure to be passed on the autostrada by two such motorcyclists as superbly equipped as these obviously are. Aboard this FJ1100 they could be cruising at 120 mph without too much bother. Its big fuel tank might mean that they could be back in Turin after only one refuelling stop. How long would it take?

In the shade with the Lateral Frame Concept showing!
Unlike the Ninja, its obvious competitor; unlike the
VF1000 Hondas with their innovative V4, but more
like the Suzuki 1100 or 1150, Yamaha ignored water
cooling which might have made the bike slimmer and
perhaps lighter. Instead they went for super refinement
in a well-practiced package. We had to wait their
750 . . .

Looks deceive. The FJ1100 is indeed a large motorcycle and it looks it. But put a rider aboard and it doesn't appear quite so. Take off, or just before, down Mulholland Highway from the Rock Store

Yamaha came first with their racer on the road. We are told that this is as close as it's possible to get in putting a V4 two-stroke Grand Prix bike into series production suitable for Joe Public to ride. What a success they have made of the RD500. Pootle around town at under say 6000 rpm and the 500 is a pussy cat. Twist the wrist and at 6500 it becomes a catapult with a claimed crankshaft horsepower of 90 peaking at 8500. *Above* Early morning at Tolworth 'tower', south London. *Right* Four pipe smoke before it cleared

Yamaha help run an RD500 Formula series in Italy –
popular, fast and furious it is too. Perfect control at
the chicane at Imola in April 1985. Faster cornering
certainly comes more easily if tucked away in that
fairing. Don't mistake the speed of this middleweight

A colourful patchwork crowd sits at the Villeneuve turn whilst a handful of Yamaha SuperTrophy '85 riders rush by. This corner is hard after a long, curving straight, curving to the right, then this relatively sharp left and accelerate up the hill

Above FZ750 – comes currently with the most advanced four-stroke engine in the history of the production motorcycle – shot here at Brands Hatch in early 1985. Rider is Graham Wood. Neat styling if overboard graphics and 1000 cc performance from 750. Look at all the features

Right Race preparation. The FZ750 comes with a water-cooled five-valve engine which is angled in the frame so that straightport, downdraught carburettors can be used. Just wonderful. 100 horsepower, 460 lb dry, and so much feel. Fast, it goes without saying

High tech line-up in the rain. Four Suzuki GSX-
R750s, four FZ750 Yamahas and two VF750F Hondas
ready for off at Brands Hatch for the first Superstock
race in 1985. Suzuki won but it's frankly pretty even.
Honda is allowed more mods to make then catch up.
Superstock founder Bruce Cox stands to the left of the
man in the cap